Guided Spelling™

First edition published 2009.

Guided Spelling is a trademark of Developmental Studies Center.

Developmental Studies Center
2000 Embarcadero, Suite 305
Oakland, CA 94606-5300
(800) 666-7270, fax: (510) 464-3670
www.devstu.org

ISBN-13: 978-1-59892-123-6
ISBN-10: 1-59892-123-1

Printed in the United States of America

1 2 3 4 5 6 7 8 9 10 MLY 18 17 16 15 14 13 12 11 10 09

Contents

Guided Spelling Lessons

Short Vowels; Frequently Misspelled Words

NEW WORDS

____	*1. catch	Catch the ball when I throw it to you.
____	*2. spend	I spend at least 30 minutes every day reading for pleasure.
____	*3. skills	My batting skills have improved since I've been practicing.
____	*4. pond	My friend and I like to catch and release frogs at the pond.
____	*5. lunches	We carried our lunches in our backpacks.
____	*6. tracks	The train tracks went through the center of town.
____	*7. badge	The police officer showed us her badge when we visited the police station.
____	*8. a lot	I see that a lot of leaves have fallen.
____	9. cannot	I cannot meet you after school.
____	10. through	The train slowed before going through the tunnel.
____	11. off	Please turn off the lights before leaving the room.
____	12. field	The owl flew over the field searching for mice.
____	13. what	I wonder what time the movie starts.
____	14. young	The young deer stared at us.
____	15. spread	We spread the blanket on the grass for the picnic.

1. _____

2. _____

3. _____

4. _____

5. _____

6. _____

7. _____

8. _____

1. _____

2. _____

3. _____

4. _____

5. _____

6. _____

7. _____

8. _____

1. _____

2. _____

3. _____

4. _____

5. _____

6. _____

7. _____

8. _____

1. _____

2. _____

3. _____

4. _____

5. _____

6. _____

7. _____

8. _____

Doubling with Single-syllable Words; Frequently Misspelled Words

NEW WORDS

___	*1. dropped	I accidentally dropped the dish.
___	*2. letting	Our teacher is letting us work together.
___	*3. cutting	They were cutting up some paper for a collage.
___	*4. scrubbed	The doctor scrubbed her hands before surgery.
___	*5. quitting	We will be quitting the game when it gets dark.
___	*6. setting	I was setting the dishes on the table.
___	*7. mixed	We mixed several colors to get the paint color we wanted.
___	*8. dressed	My little sister dressed her dolls.
___	9. can't	We can't walk against a red light.
___	10. don't	I don't often get to stay up late.
___	11. won't	My parents won't let me stay up late on school nights.
___	12. wanted	I wanted a game for my birthday.
___	13. touch	This material is soft to the touch.
___	14. though	She went for a walk even though it was raining.
___	15. clue	The detective needed one more clue to solve the case.

REVIEW WORDS

____ *16. lunches

____ *17. badge

____ *18. pond

____ *19. tracks

____ *20. catch

____ 21. field

____ 22. young

____ 23. cannot

____ 24. spread

____ 25. off

Challenge Words

whizzing, throbbed, knitting, waxed, juice

Week 2, Day 1

1. _____ + _____ = _____

2. _____ + _____ = _____

3. _____

4. _____

5. _____ + _____ = _____

6. _____

7. _____

8. _____

1. _____ + _____ = _____

2. _____ + _____ = _____

3. _____

4. _____

5. _____

6. _____

7. _____ + _____ = _____

8. _____

9. _____

10. _____

_____

Name: _____

1. _____ + _____ = _____

2. _____ + _____ = _____

3. _____

4. _____

5. _____

6. _____

7. _____ + _____ = _____

8. _____

9. _____

10. _____

_____

Name:

Week 2, Day 4

1. _____ + _____ = _____

2. _____ + _____ = _____

3. _____

4. _____

5. _____

6. _____

7. _____ + _____ = _____

8. _____

9. _____

10. _____

_____

Words with Long **a** Spelled **a**-consonant-**e**, **ai**, and **ay**; Frequently Misspelled Words

NEW WORDS

___	*1. space	There is space on the shelf to store more books.
___	*2. brain	The orca whale has a large brain for a marine mammal.
___	*3. clay	We used clay to form animals for the jungle diorama.
___	*4. age	We didn't know the dog's age.
___	*5. plain	Several hundred buffalo were grazing on the plain.
___	*6. sprayed	When the skunk sprayed, it smelled awful.
___	*7. Ms.	Ms. Holmes is our principal.
___	*8. Mr.	Mr. Childers teaches band to the fourth and fifth graders.
___	9. Miss	I told Miss Stanton that I would return the book tomorrow.
___	10. Mrs.	Mrs. Stewart had her class put on a play.
___	11. were	I wish we were going to the amusement park together.
___	12. where	I can never remember where I put my shoes.
___	13. skipped	She skipped softball practice Tuesday.
___	14. of course	I will help you study for the quiz, of course.
___	15. won	Our team won the game by one goal.

REVIEW WORDS

___ *16. mixed

___ *17. scrubbed

___ *18. dressed

___ *19. quitting

___ *20. setting

___ 21. though

___ 22. touch

___ 23. can't

___ 24. clue

___ 25. won't

Challenge Words

fade, upstairs, spare, strain, deaf

Week 3, Day 1

1. _____

2. _____

3. _____

4. _____

5. _____

6. _____

7. _____

8. _____

1. _____

2. _____

3. _____

4. _____

5. _____

6. _____

7. _____

8. _____

9. _____

10. _____

_____

Name:
_____

1. _____

2. _____

3. _____

4. _____

5. _____

6. _____

7. _____

8. _____

9. _____

10. _____

_____

1. _____

2. _____

3. _____

4. _____

5. _____

6. _____

7. _____

8. _____

9. _____

10. _____

_____

Polysyllabic Spelling

NEW WORDS

___	*1. finish	I will finish my homework on time.
___	*2. explain	Our teacher will explain the rules for the science fair.
___	*3. until	Don't cross the street until the light turns green.
___	*4. became	It became dark as the clouds covered the sun.
___	*5. public	The public library is open most Saturdays.
___	*6. unless	I won't go to the game unless you join me.
___	*7. plastic	I put the plastic bottle in the recycling bin.
___	*8. traffic	There was a lot of traffic on the freeway this morning.
___	9. expect	I expect to do well on the test because I studied hard.
___	10. insect	The monarch butterfly is a beautiful insect.
___	11. it's	It's going to be a warm and sunny day.
___	12. hitting	I hope to be hitting the ball out of the baseball park!
___	13. case	In case you forgot, your book is due today.
___	14. prove	The lawyer had to prove her case to the jury.
___	15. blood	Mosquitoes suck blood.

REVIEW WORDS

___ *16. sprayed

___ *17. Ms.

___ *18. clay

___ *19. space

___ *20. plain

___ 21. won

___ 22. Miss

___ 23. were

___ 24. of course

___ 25. skipped

Challenge Words

insist, entertain, demonstrate, pace, soup

Name: _____

1. _____

2. _____

3. _____

4. _____

5. _____

6. _____

7. _____

8. _____

1. _____

2. _____

3. _____

4. _____

5. _____

6. _____

7. _____

8. _____

9. _____

10. _____

_____

Name: _____

1. _____

2. _____

3. _____

4. _____

5. _____

6. _____

7. _____

8. _____

9. _____

10. _____

_____

1. _____

2. _____

3. _____

4. _____

5. _____

6. _____

7. _____

8. _____

9. _____

10. _____

_____

Syllables with Schwas

NEW WORDS

___	*1. second	He came in second in the foot race.
___	*2. ago	I got my first library card two years ago.
___	*3. upon	"Once upon a time" is the beginning of most fairy tales.
___	*4. moment	The lights went out for just a moment during the storm.
___	*5. open	The store will open at 10:00 a.m.
___	*6. hundred	A hundred monarch butterflies were clustered on a branch.
___	*7. even	Fifty is an even number.
___	*8. idea	He had an idea for his science report.
___	9. area	Our class met at the picnic area.
___	10. let's	Let's all join in and sing together.
___	11. splitting	We will be splitting up into two teams.
___	12. chair	I sat in a comfortable chair and read my book.
___	13. afraid	Some people are afraid of heights.
___	14. again	They want to see the movie again.
___	15. against	It was difficult to walk against the strong wind.

REVIEW WORDS

___ *16. finish

___ *17. public

___ *18. plastic

___ *19. unless

___ *20. explain

___ 21. prove

___ 22. expect

___ 23. it's

___ 24. blood

___ 25. hitting

Challenge Words

honest, definite, garbage, robin, threat

Week 5, Day 1

1. _____

2. _____

3. _____

4. _____

5. _____

6. _____

7. _____

8. _____

1. _____

2. _____

3. _____

4. _____

5. _____

6. _____

7. _____

8. _____

9. _____

10. _____

_____

Name: _____

1. _____

2. _____

3. _____

4. _____

5. _____

6. _____

7. _____

8. _____

9. _____

10. _____

_____

Name:

1. _____

2. _____

3. _____

4. _____

5. _____

6. _____

7. _____

8. _____

9. _____

10. _____

_____

Week 6

Name:
_____

Review of Weeks 1, 2, 3, and 4

Week 1

___ *1. skills

___ *2. spend

___ *3. a lot

___ *4. badge

___ *5. lunches

___ 6. field

___ 7. spread

___ 8. through

___ 9. young

___ 10. what

Week 2

___ *11. scrubbed

___ *12. quitting

___ *13. dropped

___ *14. cutting

___ *15. letting

___ *16. mixed

___ 17. though

___ 18. don't

___ 19. wanted

___ 20. won't

Week 3

___ *21. age

___ *22. brain

___ *23. sprayed

___ *24. Mr.

___ *25. plain

___ 26. won

___ 27. were

___ 28. of course

___ 29. where

___ 30. Mrs.

continues

REVIEW WEEK WORDS (continued)

Week 4

___ *31. became

___ *32. until

___ *33. unless

___ *34. explain

___ *35. finish

___ *36. traffic

___ 37. prove

___ 38. expect

___ 39. insect

___ 40. case

Challenge Words

Week 2 waxed, whizzing, knitting, juice, throbbed

Week 3 upstairs, deaf, spare, fade, strain

Week 4 pace, demonstrate, insist, soup, entertain

Name:

1. _____

2. _____

3. _____

4. _____

5. _____

6. _____

7. _____

8. _____

9. _____

10. _____

11. _____

12. _____

13. _____

14. _____

15. _____

1. _____

Mr. and Mrs Smith were letting us walk thruogh their feild.

2. _____

He will explain how the young insects find their food.

3. _____

Of cource we'll finnish on time unles we are interrupted.

4. _____

They scrubed the tables before serving the lunchs.

5. _____

We wo'nt be quiting practice untill the coach says it's time.

Syllables with Long e Spelled e-consonant-e, ee, ea, and y

NEW WORDS

___	*1. complete	I will complete my homework after dinner.
___	*2. keep	Her neighbor will keep her spare house key.
___	*3. least	I ride my bike to school at least once a week.
___	*4. energy	My puppy is a bundle of energy.
___	*5. between	I can't decide between the blue or the green backpack.
___	*6. reason	She gave the reason for her absence.
___	*7. probably	He probably will do well on the test because he studied hard.
___	*8. separate, separate	Separate the crayons. Put them in separate boxes.
___	9. problem	This problem requires three steps.
___	10. clapped	The audience clapped wildly after the performance.
___	11. away	I am going away to summer camp for two weeks.
___	12. program	The after-school art program is very popular.
___	13. sudden	All of a sudden the rain poured down.
___	14. either	You may play either soccer or basketball.
___	15. neither	She has neither a pen nor a pencil.

REVIEW WORDS

___ *16. upon

___ *17. second

___ *18. ago

___ *19. hundred

___ *20. moment

___ *21. even

___ 22. chair

___ 23. afraid

___ 24. splitting

___ 25. area

Challenge Words

stream, elementary, volunteer, beaver, fierce

Name: _____

1. _____

2. _____

3. _____

4. _____

5. _____

6. _____

7. _____

8. _____

1. _____

2. _____

3. _____

4. _____

5. _____

6. _____

7. _____

8. _____

9. _____

10. _____

_____

1. _____

2. _____

3. _____

4. _____

5. _____

6. _____

7. _____

8. _____

9. _____

10. _____

_____

Week 7, Day 4

1. _____

2. _____

3. _____

4. _____

5. _____

6. _____

7. _____

8. _____

9. _____

10. _____

_____

Syllables with **er**, **ir**, and **ur**

NEW WORDS

___	*1. serve	The cafeteria will serve lunch at noon.
___	*2. birth	At birth a baby elephant can weigh several hundred pounds.
___	*3. hurt	I hurt my arm in baseball practice.
___	*4. after	I'm going to see you after my piano lesson.
___	*5. firm	She is firm about her decision to try out for the team.
___	*6. return	He will return his library books tomorrow.
___	*7. whether	She wondered whether her parents would let her stay up.
___	*8. whenever	My dog barks whenever the doorbell rings.
___	9. better	He is much better at chess than his father is.
___	10. aid	The nurse gave first aid to the accident victims.
___	11. center	Her brother always wants to be the center of attention.
___	12. person	The person who spilled the milk should clean it up.
___	13. meet	We can meet after school and study for the quiz.
___	14. America	South America and Africa are separated by the Atlantic Ocean.
___	15. shoulder	She hung the purse over her shoulder.

REVIEW WORDS

___ *16. reason

___ *17. complete

___ *18. keep

___ *19. least

___ *20. probably

___ *21. separate (2)

___ 22. either

___ 23. away

___ 24. neither

___ 25. problem

Challenge Words

servant, precious, skirt, hammer, burst

Week 8, Day 1

Name: _____

1. _____

2. _____

3. _____

4. _____

5. _____

6. _____

7. _____

8. _____

Name:

1. _____

2. _____

3. _____

4. _____

5. _____

6. _____

7. _____

8. _____

9. _____

10. _____

_____

1. _____

2. _____

3. _____

4. _____

5. _____

6. _____

7. _____

8. _____

9. _____

10. _____

_____

1. _____

2. _____

3. _____

4. _____

5. _____

6. _____

7. _____

8. _____

9. _____

10. _____

_____

Name:
_____

Syllables with Long **i** Spelled **i**-consonant-**e**, **igh**, and **y**

NEW WORDS

___ *1. size   The store has those shoes in my size.

___ *2. fight   We heard two cats in a fight last night.

___ *3. shy   Sometimes I'm shy and don't want to speak to the whole class.

___ *4. decide   I need to decide what I will wear tomorrow.

___ *5. fright   The actor at the haunted house gave us a fright.

___ *6. all right   I'll be all right in this heat after I've had some water.

___ *7. ice   We added ice so the drinks would be cold.

___ *8. type   He prefers the seedless type of orange.

___ 9. strike   She swung at the pitch and missed; it was a strike.

___ 10. beyond   The stream is just beyond that grove of trees.

___ 11. science   In science class we learned about the molten rock under the Earth's surface.

___ 12. clear   The sky was clear and bright.

___ 13. further   We read further in the book because it was so interesting.

___ 14. among   There are too many weeds among the flowers.

___ 15. behind   Don't fall behind; we must all stay together.

Name: _____

REVIEW WORDS

____ *16. return

____ *17. whenever

____ *18. whether

____ *19. birth

____ *20. firm

____ 21. center

____ 22. better

____ 23. shoulder

____ 24. America

____ 25. meet

Challenge Words

handsome, tide, mighty, sunshine, knight

Name: _____

1. _____

2. _____

3. _____

4. _____

5. _____

6. _____

7. _____

8. _____

1. _____

2. _____

3. _____

4. _____

5. _____

6. _____

7. _____

8. _____

9. _____

10. _____

_____

Name: _____

1. _____

2. _____

3. _____

4. _____

5. _____

6. _____

7. _____

8. _____

9. _____

10. _____

_____

1. _____

2. _____

3. _____

4. _____

5. _____

6. _____

7. _____

8. _____

9. _____

10. _____

_____

Drop e Generalization

NEW WORDS

___	*1. waving	The ship's passengers were waving good-bye.
___	*2. traded	They traded the books they had just read.
___	*3. smiling	My friend is usually happy and is often smiling.
___	*4. located	The movie theater is located near the bookstore.
___	*5. provided	The teacher provided us with art paper.
___	*6. escaping	They don't want the lizard escaping from its cage.
___	*7. dividing	We were dividing the crackers between us.
___	*8. together	They walked home together.
___	9. certain	She is certain that she returned the book.
___	10. modern	Computers are a modern way of writing.
___	11. history	We studied the history of our town.
___	12. never	I never go bike riding without wearing a helmet.
___	13. side	The dolphin swam along the side of the boat.
___	14. become	Ducklings quickly become larger.
___	15. believe	I believe the concert begins at 7:00 p.m.

REVIEW WORDS

____ *16. fight

____ *17. size

____ *18. ice

____ *19. decide

____*20. all right

____ 21. clear

____ 22. strike

____ 23. further

____ 24. science

____ 25. among

Challenge Words

admired, treasure, relax, advising, decorating

Name: _____

1. _____ + _____ = _____

2. _____ + _____ = _____

3. _____

4. _____

5. _____ + _____ = _____

6. _____

7. _____

8. _____

1. _____ + _____ = _____

2. _____ + _____ = _____

3. _____

4. _____

5. _____

6. _____

7. _____ + _____ = _____

8. _____

9. _____

10. _____

_____

1. _____ + _____ = _____

2. _____ + _____ = _____

3. _____

4. _____

5. _____

6. _____

7. _____ + _____ = _____

8. _____

9. _____

10. _____

_____

1. _____ + _____ = _____

2. _____ + _____ = _____

3. _____

4. _____

5. _____

6. _____

7. _____ + _____ = _____

8. _____

9. _____

10. _____

_____

Syllables with Long **o** Spelled **o**-consonant-**e**, **oa**, and **ow**

NEW WORDS

___	*1. those	She likes those red apples.
___	*2. coast	They sailed along the rocky coast.
___	*3. known	I haven't known him long.
___	*4. follow	My dog loves to follow me.
___	*5. wrote	He wrote a letter to his grandparents.
___	*6. approach	The biologist will approach the tree snake cautiously.
___	*7. growth	There was a lot of growth in our garden this summer.
___	*8. yellow	The daisy was a bright, cheerful yellow.
___	9. spoke	I spoke to my friend on the telephone.
___	10. everything	The bus holds everything we need for our trip.
___	11. surface	The pool toys were floating on the surface.
___	12. slightly	This swimsuit is slightly damp.
___	13. saved	Her catch saved the game for her team.
___	14. dance	We learned to dance in P.E. class.
___	15. breakfast	I like fruit and cereal for breakfast.

REVIEW WORDS

____ *16. escaping

____ *17. dividing

____ *18. traded

____ *19. together

____ *20. provided

____ 21. history

____ 22. side

____ 23. never

____ 24. certain

____ 25. believe

Challenge Words

meadow, stroke, microscope, swallow, float

Name:
_____

1. _____

2. _____

3. _____

4. _____

5. _____

6. _____

7. _____

8. _____

1. _____

2. _____

3. _____

4. _____

5. _____

6. _____

7. _____

8. _____

9. _____

10. _____

_____

Name: _____

1. _____

2. _____

3. _____

4. _____

5. _____

6. _____

7. _____

8. _____

9. _____

10. _____

_____

1. _____

2. _____

3. _____

4. _____

5. _____

6. _____

7. _____

8. _____

9. _____

10. _____

_____

Review of Weeks 5, 7, 8, 9, and 10

Week 5

____ *1. even

____ *2. open

____ *3. idea

____ *4. hundred

____ *5. second

____ 6. let's

____ 7. against

____ 8. afraid

____ 9. again

____ 10. area

Week 7

____ *11. probably

____ *12. energy

____ *13. least

____ *14. separate (2)

____ *15. between

____ 16. sudden

____ 17. problem

____ 18. clapped

____ 19. either

____ 20. program

Week 8

____ *21. hurt

____ *22. serve

____ *23. return

____ *24. whenever

____ *25. after

____ 26. America

____ 27. aid

____ 28. center

____ 29. shoulder

____ 30. person

continues

REVIEW WEEK WORDS (continued)

Week 9

___ *31. all right

___ *32. shy

___ *33. fright

___ *34. decide

___ *35. type

___ 36. further

___ 37. beyond

___ 38. among

___ 39. science

___ 40. behind

Week 10

___ *41. smiling

___ *42. escaping

___ *43. waving

___ *44. located

___ *45. dividing

___ *46. together

___ 47. become

___ 48. modern

___ 49. believe

___ 50. history

Challenge Words

Week 5 robin, definite, threat, honest, garbage

Week 7 elementary, beaver, fierce, volunteer, stream

Week 8 burst, servant, precious, hammer, skirt

Week 9 handsome, tide, knight, mighty, sunshine

Week 10 decorating, relax, admired, treasure, advising

Name: _____

1. _____

2. _____

3. _____

4. _____

5. _____

6. _____

7. _____

8. _____

9. _____

10. _____

11. _____

12. _____

13. _____

14. _____

15. _____

1. _____

They went to aide the person who had been hirt.

2. _____

Everyone claped after the sience program about enurgy.

3. _____

The book is probubly locatted on the shelf behind you.

4. _____

Lets deside which project to work on together.

5. _____

Their friends were smileing and waveing as they drove away to retern home.

6. _____

The sudden noise gave a fright to the shy little mouse.

Name:
_____

Syllables with **or** and **ore**; Syllables with **ar**

NEW WORDS

____	*1. born	He was born in September.
____	*2. shore	We collected seashells at the shore.
____	*3. start	The race will start at the library.
____	*4. form	We will form the clay into pots.
____	*5. mark	He will mark the board for the carpenter.
____	*6. corner	The store is at the corner.
____	*7. forest	The deer wandered through the forest.
____	*8. began	We began the school day with a math review.
____	9. knowledge	His grandfather has a lot of knowledge about gardening.
____	10. matter	I will finish no matter how long it takes.
____	11. wife	My uncle's wife is my aunt.
____	12. wasting	I am very careful about not wasting water.
____	13. alone	The dog was alone in the backyard.
____	14. another	I would like to have another tropical fish.
____	15. brother	Her brother will drive her to her friend's house.

REVIEW WORDS

___ *16. yellow

___ *17. known

___ *18. follow

___ *19. coast

___ *20. those

___ *21. growth

___ 22. saved

___ 23. everything

___ 24. dance

___ 25. surface

Challenge Words

fort, orbit, argue, remind, target

Name:

1. _____

2. _____

3. _____

4. _____

5. _____

6. _____

7. _____

8. _____

1. _____

2. _____

3. _____

4. _____

5. _____

6. _____

7. _____

8. _____

9. _____

10. _____

_____

Name:
_____

1. _____

2. _____

3. _____

4. _____

5. _____

6. _____

7. _____

8. _____

9. _____

10. _____

_____

1. _____

2. _____

3. _____

4. _____

5. _____

6. _____

7. _____

8. _____

9. _____

10. _____

_____

Syllables with Long **u** and Sound /o͞o/

NEW WORDS

___	*1. huge	The humpback whale is a huge mammal.
___	*2. tool	A hammer is a useful tool to have around the house.
___	*3. include	The activity will include everyone.
___	*4. drew	He drew a beautiful picture of a butterfly.
___	*5. used to	I'm used to going to bed early.
___	*6. produce	The new factory will produce new cars.
___	*7. afternoon	During vacation we do crafts in the afternoon.
___	*8. different	There were different kinds of stories in the book.
___	9. figure	The square is a four-sided figure.
___	10. tonight	They will be stargazing tonight.
___	11. priced	The store offered low-priced office supplies.
___	12. shown	We were shown to our seats at the concert.
___	13. force	She hit the baseball with great force.
___	14. view	The view of the valley was breathtaking.
___	15. police	The police were directing traffic.

Name: _____

REVIEW WORDS

____ *16. mark

____ *17. forest

____ *18. shore

____ *19. began

____ *20. corner

____ 21. knowledge

____ 22. wife

____ 23. matter

____ 24. another

____ 25. brother

Challenge Words

restaurant, proof, introduce, cured, jewels

Name: _____

1. _____

2. _____

3. _____

4. _____

5. _____

6. _____

7. _____

8. _____

1. _____

2. _____

3. _____

4. _____

5. _____

6. _____

7. _____

8. _____

9. _____

10. _____

_____

Name: _____

1. _____

2. _____

3. _____

4. _____

5. _____

6. _____

7. _____

8. _____

9. _____

10. _____

_____

1. _____

2. _____

3. _____

4. _____

5. _____

6. _____

7. _____

8. _____

9. _____

10. _____

_____

Name: _____

Syllables -*tion* and -*sion*

NEW WORDS

___	*1. action	The movie was full of action.
___	*2. discussion	We had a discussion about the problem.
___	*3. television	Mom turns off the television when we do our homework.
___	*4. information	The ranger gave us information about animals.
___	*5. attention	Pay attention when the instructions are given.
___	*6. section	They sat in the front section.
___	*7. decision	I will decide now and stick to my decision.
___	*8. question	I have a question about the assignment.
___	9. future	A new soccer field is planned for the future.
___	10. driving	My sister will be driving home from college.
___	11. below	The temperature dipped below freezing this morning.
___	12. party	We planned a party for my grandparents.
___	13. tube	They floated down the river on an inner tube.
___	14. answer	I knew the answer to the question.
___	15. period	The grading period ended in November.

REVIEW WORDS

___ *16. tool

___ *17. huge

___ *18. afternoon

___ *19. used to

___ *20. drew

___ 21. priced

___ 22. police

___ 23. view

___ 24. force

___ 25. shown

Challenge Words

canyon, emotions, protection, reward, vision

Name: _____

1. _____

2. _____

3. _____

4. _____

5. _____

6. _____

7. _____

8. _____

1. _____

2. _____

3. _____

4. _____

5. _____

6. _____

7. _____

8. _____

9. _____

10. _____

_____

Name: _____

1. _____

2. _____

3. _____

4. _____

5. _____

6. _____

7. _____

8. _____

9. _____

10. _____

_____

Week 15, Day 4

1. _____

2. _____

3. _____

4. _____

5. _____

6. _____

7. _____

8. _____

9. _____

10. _____

_____

Name: _____

Spelling Possessives

NEW WORDS

___	*1. today's	They will have today's spelling test after lunch.
___	*2. nation's	One of our nation's symbols is the bald eagle.
___	*3. nations'	The nations' leaders discussed how to protect their shared coastline.
___	*4. children's	The children's zoo has an animal nursery.
___	*5. tree's	Our one tree's branches shade our backyard.
___	*6. trees'	Many trees' canopies keep the rain forest cool and damp.
___	*7. women's	The women's softball tournament will be this weekend.
___	*8. village	The village was located in a beautiful valley.
___	9. language	My father speaks more than one language.
___	10. window	Shut the window to keep the bees out.
___	11. morning	I love to wake up early in the morning.
___	12. threw	He threw the ball over the fence.
___	13. population	The population of the school has increased this year.
___	14. parents	Her parents walk her to school every day.
___	15. island	There is an island in the middle of the lake.

REVIEW WORDS

___ *16. discussion   ___ *21. action

___ *17. decision   ___ 22. below

___ *18. television   ___ 23. period

___ *19. information   ___ 24. party

___ *20. question   ___ 25. driving

Challenge Words

attic, envelope, wander, collar, ticket

Week 16, Day 1

Name: _____

1. _____

2. _____

3. _____

4. _____

5. _____

6. _____

7. _____

8. _____

Week 16, Day 2

1. _____

2. _____

3. _____

4. _____

5. _____

6. _____

7. _____

8. _____

9. _____

10. _____

_____

1. _____

2. _____

3. _____

4. _____

5. _____

6. _____

7. _____

8. _____

9. _____

10. _____

_____

1. _____

2. _____

3. _____

4. _____

5. _____

6. _____

7. _____

8. _____

9. _____

10. _____

_____

Syllables with /ŏ͝o/ Spelled **oo**;
Syllables with /ou/ Spelled **ou** and **ow**

NEW WORDS

___	*1. shook	I shook my head in disbelief.
___	*2. round	Their kitchen table is round.
___	*3. cow	The cow grazed in the meadow.
___	*4. wool	Most of my winter sweaters are made from wool.
___	*5. amount	The amount of flour needed is two cups.
___	*6. flower	A rose is a fragrant flower.
___	*7. mountain	There was snow on the mountain year round.
___	*8. allow	Does the museum allow dogs?
___	9. temperature	We set the oven temperature at 375 degrees.
___	10. order	I placed my lunch order at the counter.
___	11. cool	It became cool at sunset.
___	12. education	My sister will finish her college education this spring.
___	13. year's	This year's rainfall has been less than predicted.
___	14. cover	The back cover had information about the author.
___	15. discover	You'll discover many tiny creatures in a garden.

REVIEW WORDS

___ *16. nations'

___ *17. women's

___ *18. children's

___ *19. nation's

___ *20. tree's

___ 21. threw

___ 22. parents

___ 23. window

___ 24. language

___ 25. population

Challenge Words

playground, avenue, aloud, tower, owl

Name: _____

1. _____

2. _____

3. _____

4. _____

5. _____

6. _____

7. _____

8. _____

1. _____

2. _____

3. _____

4. _____

5. _____

6. _____

7. _____

8. _____

9. _____

10. _____

_____

Name: _____

1. _____

2. _____

3. _____

4. _____

5. _____

6. _____

7. _____

8. _____

9. _____

10. _____

_____

1. _____

2. _____

3. _____

4. _____

5. _____

6. _____

7. _____

8. _____

9. _____

10. _____

_____

Name: _____

Review of Weeks 11, 13, 14, 15, and 16

Week 11

___ *1. wrote

___ *2. known

___ *3. approach

___ *4. follow

___ *5. coast

___ 6. surface

___ 7. spoke

___ 8. saved

___ 9. slightly

___ 10. breakfast

Week 13

___ *11. shore

___ *12. born

___ *13. forest

___ *14. began

___ *15. mark

___ 16. alone

___ 17. knowledge

___ 18. wasting

___ 19. brother

___ 20. another

Week 14

___ *21. afternoon

___ *22. huge

___ *23. include

___ *24. produce

___ *25. used to

___ *26. different

___ 27. force

___ 28. figure

___ 29. police

___ 30. tonight

continues

Name: _____

REVIEW WEEK WORDS (continued)

Week 15

____ *31. television

____ *32. attention

____ *33. discussion

____ *34. decision

____ *35. section

____ *36. question

____ 37. tube

____ 38. period

____ 39. answer

____ 40. future

Week 16

____ *41. nation's (*the nation's capital*)

____ *42. trees' (*these trees' apples*)

____ *43. today's

____ *44. village

____ *45. children's

____ *46. tree's (*this tree's leaves*)

____ 47. population

____ 48. island

____ 49. morning

____ 50. parents

Challenge Words

Week 11 float, stroke, meadow, microscope, swallow

Week 13 orbit, target, remind, argue, fort

Week 14 jewels, cured, introduce, restaurant, proof

Week 15 reward, canyon, protection, emotions, vision

Week 16 ticket, envelope, wander, attic, collar

Name: _____

1. _____

2. _____

3. _____

4. _____

5. _____

6. _____

7. _____

8. _____

9. _____

10. _____

11. _____

12. _____

13. _____

14. _____

15. _____

1. _____

That nations' population passed the one million mark.

2. _____

They gained knowlage by paying attension to other students' ansers.

3. _____

The iland off the coast had a beautiful sandy shor.

4. _____

The childrens parents' make brekfast every morning.

5. _____

We saw on telavision that todays weather will be warm in the afternoon

_____

and slightly cooler tonite.

6. _____

I use to follow my bruther wherever he went.

Change y to i Generalization

NEW WORDS

___	*1.	replied	She replied to the question.
___	*2.	stories	The librarian reads children's stories aloud.
___	*3.	copying	I will be copying your address into my book.
___	*4.	married	Their parents were married in Paris.
___	*5.	babies	The babies were sleeping in the nursery.
___	*6.	activities	There were many activities at the school carnival.
___	*7.	supplies	I need to get new school supplies.
___	*8.	picture	My grandmother put my picture on her mantel.
___	9.	nature	We hiked on the nature trail to the redwood trees.
___	10.	room	There is plenty of room for everyone.
___	11.	conditions	The weather conditions were excellent for skiing.
___	12.	streets'	Our city streets' dividing lines need repainting.
___	13.	understood	They understood all of the rules of the game.
___	14.	sugar	We made lemonade from lemon, water, and sugar.
___	15.	worry	Don't worry about the test; I'm sure you did well.

REVIEW WORDS

___ *16. allow

___ *17. flower

___ *18. mountain

___ *19. cow

___ *20. shook

___ 21. cover

___ 22. order

___ 23. temperature

___ 24. discover

___ 25. education

Challenge Words

groceries, fasten, alphabet, victories, relying

Name: _____

1. _____ + _____ = _____

2. _____ + _____ = _____

3. _____

4. _____

5. _____ + _____ = _____

6. _____

7. _____

8. _____

1. _____ + _____ = _____

2. _____ + _____ = _____

3. _____

4. _____

5. _____

6. _____

7. _____ + _____ = _____

8. _____

9. _____

10. _____

_____

Name: _____

1. _____ + _____ = _____

2. _____ + _____ = _____

3. _____

4. _____

5. _____

6. _____

7. _____ + _____ = _____

8. _____

9. _____

10. _____

_____

1. _____ + _____ = _____

2. _____ + _____ = _____

3. _____

4. _____

5. _____

6. _____

7. _____ + _____ = _____

8. _____

9. _____

10. _____

_____

Syllables Ending in Consonant-l-e and Consonant-a-l

NEW WORDS

___ *1. table   We set the table for dinner.

___ *2. several   There are several peaches in the bowl.

___ *3. level   Some areas of Death Valley are below sea level.

___ *4. example   This painting is an example of the artist's early work.

___ *5. animal   The koala is an animal native to Australia.

___ *6. travel   My aunt loves to travel to South America.

___ *7. bicycle   She rode her bicycle to her friend's house.

___ *8. general   In general, the bus is here by 8:30 a.m.

___ 9. single   She took a single helping.

___ 10. addition   Their school will have an addition of six classrooms.

___ 11. stones'   We gathered many stones. The stones' weight was too great for the pickup truck.

___ 12. around   We will leave for the game around 4:00 p.m.

___ 13. libraries   There are libraries in our district schools.

___ 14. receive   He will receive an award for his science project.

___ 15. iron   The gate was made of iron.

REVIEW WORDS

____ *16. activities

____ *17. picture

____ *18. stories

____ *19. supplies

____ *20. married

____ 21. conditions

____ 22. worry

____ 23. understood

____ 24. room

____ 25. streets'

Challenge Words

colonial, label, whistle, saddle, sandwich

1. _____

2. _____

3. _____

4. _____

5. _____

6. _____

7. _____

8. _____

1. _____

2. _____

3. _____

4. _____

5. _____

6. _____

7. _____

8. _____

9. _____

10. _____

_____

1. _____

2. _____

3. _____

4. _____

5. _____

6. _____

7. _____

8. _____

9. _____

10. _____

_____

1. _____

2. _____

3. _____

4. _____

5. _____

6. _____

7. _____

8. _____

9. _____

10. _____

_____

Syllables with **oi** and **oy**;
Syllables with /aw/ Spelled **au**, **aw**, and **a**

NEW WORDS

___	*1. soil	The soil was perfect for growing vegetables.
___	*2. destroy	A big fire can destroy many homes.
___	*3. fault	It was her fault that the dog got out of the yard.
___	*4. law	The law requires you to wear your seatbelt.
___	*5. already	She has already graduated from high school.
___	*6. all ready	The dinner was all ready, so we sat down to eat.
___	*7. although	She did not respond, although she knew the answer.
___	*8. family	We will have a family reunion at the park.
___	9. result	Your hard work will result in a good grade.
___	10. lake's	The lake's shoreline is steep and rocky.
___	11. power	The house is heated with solar power.
___	12. factories	Many car factories are located nearby.
___	13. little	The little books were in a basket.
___	14. machine	The mechanic used a machine to lift the car.
___	15. taught	I taught my brother how to write his name.

REVIEW WORDS

____ *16. several

____ *17. travel

____ *18. example

____ *19. general

____ *20. table

____ 21. libraries

____ 22. around

____ 23. single

____ 24. stones'

____ 25. receive

Challenge Words

false, dinosaur, coins, straw, altogether

Name: _____

1. _____

2. _____

3. _____

4. _____

5. _____

6. _____

7. _____

8. _____

1. _____

2. _____

3. _____

4. _____

5. _____

6. _____

7. _____

8. _____

9. _____

10. _____

_____

Name: _____

1. _____

2. _____

3. _____

4. _____

5. _____

6. _____

7. _____

8. _____

9. _____

10. _____

_____

1. _____

2. _____

3. _____

4. _____

5. _____

6. _____

7. _____

8. _____

9. _____

10. _____

_____

Name: _____

Prefixes *un-*, *re-*, and *dis-*

NEW WORDS

___ *1. unimportant   This fact is unimportant to the case.

___ *2. recycle   We recycle plastic jars, aluminum cans, and paper.

___ *3. disagree   Sometimes I disagree with my mom about what I will wear.

___ *4. unusual   We knew there was something wrong because the car was making an unusual sound.

___ *5. recharge   We must recharge the electric car every one hundred miles.

___ *6. disconnected   The family moved and had the telephone disconnected.

___ *7. disobey   If you disobey the rules, you won't get to play in the game.

___ *8. doctor   His doctor advised him to exercise.

___ 9. million   There seemed to be a million stars in the sky.

___ 10. thousand   Ten one-hundred-dollar bills equal one thousand dollars.

___ 11. memories   I have wonderful memories of my camping vacation.

___ 12. total   The total amount he owed was on the bill.

___ 13. noise   There was a faint chirping noise coming from the nest.

___ 14. weigh   She stepped on the scale to weigh herself.

___ 15. neighbor   We brought our new neighbor a plant.

REVIEW WORDS

___ *16. destroy
___ *17. all ready
___ *18. law
___ *19. already
___ *20. although

___ 21. machine
___ 22. result
___ 23. little
___ 24. lake's
___ 25. factories

Challenge Words

legend, unconscious, guest, disapprove, reawaken

Name: _____

1. _____

2. _____

3. _____

4. _____

5. _____

6. _____

7. _____

8. _____

1. _____

2. _____

3. _____

4. _____

5. _____

6. _____

7. _____

8. _____

9. _____

10. _____

_____

Name: _____

1. _____ .

2. _____

3. _____

4. _____

5. _____

6. _____

7. _____

8. _____

9. _____

10. _____

_____

1. _____

2. _____

3. _____

4. _____

5. _____

6. _____

7. _____

8. _____

9. _____

10. _____

_____

Name: _____

Suffixes -*ful*, -*less*, and -*ness*

NEW WORDS

___	*1. thoughtful	It was so thoughtful of you to send me a card.
___	*2. colorless	Water is a clear liquid; it is colorless.
___	*3. brightness	We wore sunglasses due to the brightness of the sun.
___	*4. fearful	I am very fearful of spiders.
___	*5. tasteless	The soup had no flavor; it was tasteless.
___	*6. friendliness	She gets along well with people and is known for her friendliness.
___	*7. mouthful	The baby had a mouthful of crackers.
___	*8. office	The school office is located near the library.
___	9. president	The president of the university spoke to the graduating class.
___	10. colonies	There were ant colonies located on the hill.
___	11. physical	I need a physical exam before I can join the team.
___	12. audience	The audience clapped wildly for the performers.
___	13. uninteresting	That story was very uninteresting; I didn't enjoy it at all.
___	14. height	I have grown in height this year; I'm taller than I was last year.
___	15. weight	The veterinarian recommends that our cat lose some weight.

Name: _____

REVIEW WORDS

____ *16. recycle

____ *17. unusual

____ *18. doctor

____ *19. disobey

____ *20. unimportant

____ 21. thousand

____ 22. neighbor

____ 23. memories

____ 24. noise

____ 25. million

Challenge Words

politeness, sorrowful, canoe, restless, motionless

1. _____

2. _____

3. _____

4. _____

5. _____

6. _____

7. _____

8. _____

1. _____

2. _____

3. _____

4. _____

5. _____

6. _____

7. _____

8. _____

9. _____

10. _____

_____

Name: _____

1. _____

2. _____

3. _____

4. _____

5. _____

6. _____

7. _____

8. _____

9. _____

10. _____

_____

1. _____

2. _____

3. _____

4. _____

5. _____

6. _____

7. _____

8. _____

9. _____

10. _____

_____

Week 24

Name:

Review of Weeks 17, 19, 20, 21, and 22

Week 17

___ *1. amount

___ *2. round

___ *3. flower

___ *4. mountain

___ *5. wool

___ 6. year's (*this year's weather*)

___ 7. discover

___ 8. temperature

___ 9. cool

___ 10. cover

Week 19

___ *11. copying

___ *12. babies

___ *13. supplies

___ *14. activities

___ *15. replied

___ 16. sugar

___ 17. nature

___ 18. worry

___ 19. understood

___ 20. conditions

Week 20

___ *21. travel

___ *22. several

___ *23. animal

___ *24. level

___ *25. general

___ *26. bicycle

___ 27. libraries

___ 28. iron

___ 29. addition

___ 30. receive

continues

REVIEW WEEK WORDS (continued)

Week 21

___ *31. soil

___ *32. already

___ *33. fault

___ *34. family

___ *35. all ready

___ 36. result

___ 37. machine

___ 38. power

___ 39. taught

___ 40. factories

Week 22

___ *41. recharge

___ *42. recycle

___ *43. disobey

___ *44. disagree

___ *45. unusual

___ *46. disconnected

___ 47. thousand

___ 48. million

___ 49. weigh

___ 50. total

Challenge Words

Week 17 owl, avenue, playground, aloud, tower

Week 19 groceries, alphabet, fasten, victories, relying

Week 20 saddle, sandwich, colonial, whistle, label

Week 21 false, coins, straw, dinosaur, altogether

Week 22 reawaken, legend, guest, unconscious, disapprove

Name:

1. _____

2. _____

3. _____

4. _____

5. _____

6. _____

7. _____

8. _____

9. _____

10. _____

11. _____

12. _____

13. _____

14. _____

15. _____

1. _____

Factaries use wool from animils such as sheep and alpacas to produce clothing.

2. _____

Next summer their family will traval a thousend miles by bycicle.

3. _____

This years' cool temperatures have been very ususual.

4. _____

She disconectted the powar cord from the mechine.

5. _____

We've all ready had several activities to promote recycleing.

6. _____

The teacher taught them about the soil condisions and the amout of water

_____

needed to grow tropical flours.

Prefixes *non-*, *mis-*, and *pre-*

NEW WORDS

____ *1. nonfiction   My favorite nonfiction books are about animals.

____ *2. misunderstanding   We had a misunderstanding about what time the concert started, so we arrived late.

____ *3. pregame   The pregame show was a marching band performance.

____ *4. nonhuman   Robots can seem alive, but they are nonhuman.

____ *5. misbehaved   My little brother misbehaved at the concert, so Dad took him out to the lobby.

____ *6. precooked   He precooked the stew and reheated it before supper.

____ *7. misspelled   I misspelled your name by mistake.

____ *8. student   A new student joined our class this week.

____ 9. direction   The plane was headed in a southerly direction.

____ 10. special   The store had a special offer on electronic equipment.

____ 11. always   I will always be there to help you.

____ 12. restudy   I will restudy and take the test again.

____ 13. wireless   The wireless connection was very convenient.

____ 14. danger   There was a danger sign in front of the rock slide.

____ 15. ahead   I see the lights of the town up ahead.

REVIEW WORDS

____ *16. fearful

____ *17. thoughtful

____ *18. colorless

____ *19. office

____ *20. friendliness

____ 21. colonies

____ 22. president

____ 23. weight

____ 24. physical

____ 25. audience

Challenge Words

misfortune, berries, preshrunk, nonpoisonous, closet

1. _____

2. _____

3. _____

4. _____

5. _____

6. _____

7. _____

8. _____

1. _____

2. _____

3. _____

4. _____

5. _____

6. _____

7. _____

8. _____

9. _____

10. _____

_____

Name: _____

1. _____

2. _____

3. _____

4. _____

5. _____

6. _____

7. _____

8. _____

9. _____

10. _____

_____

1. _____

2. _____

3. _____

4. _____

5. _____

6. _____

7. _____

8. _____

9. _____

10. _____

_____

Name:

_____

Unusual Plurals

NEW WORDS

___	*1. life	We studied the life cycle of the monarch butterfly.
___	*2. lives	Health professionals save lives every day.
___	*3. halves	Cut the tomatoes into halves.
___	*4. ourselves	We need to do this project by ourselves.
___	*5. teeth	She gets her teeth cleaned at the dentist's office.
___	*6. sheep	The sheep grazed on the hillside.
___	*7. potatoes	I love roasted potatoes for dinner.
___	*8. except	I can go swimming every day except Monday.
___	9. environment	Lions live in a hot and dry environment.
___	10. join	They will join hands and dance in a circle.
___	11. disappear	The plane flew into the clouds and seemed to disappear.
___	12. darkness	Most owls hunt only when darkness comes.
___	13. secret	They kept their mother's present a secret until her birthday.
___	14. valley	A stream ran through the valley.
___	15. control	He learned how to control his dog at dog training class.

Name: ____

REVIEW WORDS

___ *16. nonfiction
___ *17. misbehaved
___ *18. misunderstanding
___ *19. pregame
___ *20. nonhuman

___ 21. direction
___ 22. ahead
___ 23. always
___ 24. special
___ 25. wireless

Challenge Words

salmon, tomatoes, oxen, volcanoes, calves

Name: _____

1. _____

2. _____

3. _____

4. _____

5. _____

6. _____

7. _____

8. _____

1. _____

2. _____

3. _____

4. _____

5. _____

6. _____

7. _____

8. _____

9. _____

10. _____

_____

Name: _____

1. _____

2. _____

3. _____

4. _____

5. _____

6. _____

7. _____

8. _____

9. _____

10. _____

_____

1. _____

2. _____

3. _____

4. _____

5. _____

6. _____

7. _____

8. _____

9. _____

10. _____

_____

Name: _____

Doubling with Polysyllabic Words

NEW WORDS

___	*1. beginning	The table of contents is at the beginning of the book.
___	*2. controlled	He controlled the toy car with a remote control device.
___	*3. happened	Her birthday happened to fall on the last day of school.
___	*4. forgetting	I won't be forgetting my homework tomorrow.
___	*5. remembered	She remembered to return her library book.
___	*6. maybe	I'm not sure whether I'll go; maybe I will.
___	*7. minute	We'll be finished in one minute.
___	*8. bottom	The class rode on the lake in a glass-bottom boat.
___	9. difficult	The math homework was difficult.
___	10. unnumbered	The pages of the book were unnumbered.
___	11. lateness	He has a problem with lateness; he never gets to practice on time.
___	12. misheard	I misheard the time and was late for the movie.
___	13. wives	Both wives and husbands joined in the activity.
___	14. ocean	An ocean separates North America from Asia.
___	15. lie	My dog will lie on her cushion.

REVIEW WORDS

___ *16. except

___ *17. sheep

___ *18. life

___ *19. ourselves

___ *20. potatoes

___ 21. darkness

___ 22. environment

___ 23. secret

___ 24. control

___ 25. join

Challenge Words

propeller, polish, occurred, statue, preferred

Name: _____

1. _____ + _____ = _____

2. _____ + _____ = _____

3. _____

4. _____

5. _____ + _____ = _____

6. _____

7. _____

8. _____

1. _____ + _____ = _____

2. _____ + _____ = _____

3. _____

4. _____

5. _____

6. _____

7. _____ + _____ = _____

8. _____

9. _____

10. _____

_____

Name: _____

1. _____ + _____ = _____

2. _____ + _____ = _____

3. _____

4. _____

5. _____

6. _____

7. _____ + _____ = _____

8. _____

9. _____

10. _____

_____

1. _____ + _____ = _____

2. _____ + _____ = _____

3. _____

4. _____

5. _____

6. _____

7. _____ + _____ = _____

8. _____

9. _____

10. _____

_____

Suffixes -*er*, -*or*, and -*est*

NEW WORDS

___	*1. earlier	The swimmers had practiced earlier in the day.
___	*2. cleanest	My brother has the cleanest bike of all.
___	*3. leader	The line leader guided us to the auditorium.
___	*4. actor	The actor spent many years perfecting his craft.
___	*5. easiest	That was the easiest piece of music to learn.
___	*6. teacher	The piano teacher had her students put on a recital.
___	*7. quieter	The neighborhood is quieter at night.
___	*8. notice	There was a notice on the telephone pole about a lost cat.
___	9. exact	He needed exact change for the machine.
___	10. hardness	The hardness of the ice allowed us to walk on the frozen lake.
___	11. preseason	The players practiced on the school field during the preseason.
___	12. purpose	The purpose of the meeting was to introduce the new police chief.
___	13. beginner	She is a beginner at soccer.
___	14. measure	I need to measure two cups of flour for this recipe.
___	15. wonder	I wonder if I'll get a kitten for my birthday.

REVIEW WORDS

___ *16. forgetting

___ *17. maybe

___ *18. controlled

___ *19. beginning

___ *20. remembered

___ 21. ocean

___ 22. lie

___ 23. wives

___ 24. misheard

___ 25. difficult

Challenge Words

juiciest, curious, slimmest, employer, refrigerator

Name: _____

1. _____

2. _____

3. _____

4. _____

5. _____

6. _____

7. _____

8. _____

1. _____

2. _____

3. _____

4. _____

5. _____

6. _____

7. _____

8. _____

9. _____

10. _____

_____

Name: _____

1. _____

2. _____

3. _____

4. _____

5. _____

6. _____

7. _____

8. _____

9. _____

10. _____

_____

1. _____

2. _____

3. _____

4. _____

5. _____

6. _____

7. _____

8. _____

9. _____

10. _____

_____

Word Parts -*able* and -*ible*

NEW WORDS

___	*1. washable	This baby blanket is washable.
___	*2. impossible	It was almost impossible to remove the lid from the jar.
___	*3. terrible	He had a terrible cold and stayed home from school.
___	*4. replaceable	The broken saw was replaceable; there were many others like it.
___	*5. disagreeable	She is very disagreeable; she's always arguing with people.
___	*6. vegetables	They always have vegetables for dinner.
___	*7. nonreturnable	This dress was on sale, so it is nonreturnable.
___	*8. written	The book was written by a well-known author.
___	9. summer	In the summer the evenings are long.
___	10. misplaced	My dad misplaced his car keys, so we were late to school.
___	11. forward	The car jerked forward and bumped into the curb.
___	12. unforgettable	I loved that book; it is unforgettable.
___	13. tiniest	The Chihuahua is the tiniest dog I have ever seen.
___	14. solve	We were given several math problems to solve.
___	15. serious	He was very serious about piano lessons.

REVIEW WORDS

____ *16. notice

____ *17. quieter

____ *18. leader

____ *19. easiest

____ *20. actor

____ 21. hardness

____ 22. purpose

____ 23. measure

____ 24. beginner

____ 25. wonder

Challenge Words

rescue, portable, inexcusable, reversible, disposable

Name: _____

1. _____

2. _____

3. _____

4. _____

5. _____

6. _____

7. _____

8. _____

1. _____

2. _____

3. _____

4. _____

5. _____

6. _____

7. _____

8. _____

9. _____

10. _____

_____

Name: _____

1. _____

2. _____

3. _____

4. _____

5. _____

6. _____

7. _____

8. _____

9. _____

10. _____

_____

1. _____

2. _____

3. _____

4. _____

5. _____

6. _____

7. _____

8. _____

9. _____

10. _____

_____

Name: _____

Review of Weeks 23, 25, 26, 27, and 28

Week 23

___ *1. tasteless

___ *2. thoughtful

___ *3. office

___ *4. friendliness

___ *5. brightness

___ *6. mouthful

___ 7. physical

___ 8. weight

___ 9. height

___ 10. uninteresting

Week 25

___ *11. misunderstanding

___ *12. precooked

___ *13. misspelled

___ *14. misbehaved

___ *15. student

___ *16. nonfiction

___ 17. restudy

___ 18. danger

___ 19. wireless

___ 20. special

Week 26

___ *21. teeth

___ *22. lives

___ *23. potatoes

___ *24. except

___ *25. halves

___ 26. join

___ 27. valley

___ 28. environment

___ 29. control

___ 30. disappear

continues

REVIEW WEEK WORDS (continued)

Week 27

____ *31. controlled

____ *32. bottom

____ *33. happened

____ *34. beginning

____ *35. minute

____ 36. difficult

____ 37. misheard

____ 38. unnumbered

____ 39. lateness

____ 40. ocean

Week 28

____ *41. actor

____ *42. earliest

____ *43. cleanest

____ *44. quieter

____ *45. teacher

____ 46. preseason

____ 47. exact

____ 48. measure

____ 49. beginner

____ 50. purpose

Challenge Words

Week 23 motionless, canoe, politeness, restless, sorrowful

Week 25 misfortune, nonpoisonous, berries, closet, preshrunk

Week 26 tomatoes, salmon, calves, volcanoes, oxen

Week 27 occurred, statue, propeller, polish, preferred

Week 28 slimmest, employer, juiciest, curious, refrigerator

Name: _____

1. _____

2. _____

3. _____

4. _____

5. _____

6. _____

7. _____

8. _____

9. _____

10. _____

11. _____

12. _____

13. _____

14. _____

15. _____

Name: _____

1. _____

Humans do not have teeth at the begining of their lifes.

2. _____

When a nonfiction book is too difficult, it can seem uninteresting.

3. _____

After the teachor spoke about lateness, they tried to arrive earlyer.

4. _____

Watch these potatos' disapear mouthful by mouthful.

5. _____

Astronomers can teach students' to mesure the brighness of each star.

6. _____

I mispelled a word, so I had to re studdy it.

Dictionary and Personal Word List

Dictionary and Personal Word List

Name: _____

A

___action
___activities
___actor
___addition
___afraid
___after
___afternoon
___again
___against
___age
___ago
___ahead
___aid
___allow
___all ready
___all right
___alone
___a lot
___already
___although
___always
___America
___among
___amount

___animal
___another
___answer
___approach
___area
___around
___attention
___audience
___away

_____
_____
_____
_____
_____
_____
_____
_____
_____

B

___babies
___badge
___became
___become

___began
___beginner
___beginning
___behind
___believe
___below
___better
___between
___beyond
___bicycle
___birth
___blood
___born
___bottom
___brain
___breakfast
___brightness
___brother

_____
_____
_____
_____
_____
_____
_____

Name: _____

C

— cannot
— can't
— case
— catch
— center
— certain
— chair
— children's
— clapped
— clay
— cleanest
— clear
— clue
— coast
— colonies
— colorless
— complete
— conditions
— control
— controlled
— cool
— copying
— corner
— cover

— cow
— cutting
_____
_____
_____
_____
_____
_____
_____
_____

D

— dance
— danger
— darkness
— decide
— decision
— destroy
— different
— difficult
— direction
— disagree
— disagreeable
— disappear

— disconnected
— discover
— discussion
— disobey
— dividing
— doctor
— don't
— dressed
— drew
— driving
— dropped
_____
_____
_____
_____
_____
_____
_____

E

— earlier
— easiest
— education
— either
— energy

Dictionary and Personal Word List

Name: _____

___ environment

___ escaping

___ even

___ everything

___ exact

___ example

___ except

___ expect

___ explain

_____

_____

_____

_____

_____

F

___ factories

___ family

___ fault

___ fearful

___ field

___ fight

___ figure

___ finish

___ firm

___ flower

___ follow

___ force

___ forest

___ forgetting

___ form

___ forward

___ friendliness

___ fright

___ further

___ future

_____

_____

_____

_____

_____

_____

_____

_____

G

___ general

___ growth

_____

_____

_____

H

___ halves

___ happened

___ hardness

___ height

___ history

___ hitting

___ huge

___ hundred

___ hurt

_____

_____

_____

I, J, K

___ ice

___ idea

___ impossible

___ include

___ information

___ insect

___ iron

___ island

___ it's

___ join

Name: _____

—keep
—knowledge
—known

_____
_____
_____
_____
_____
_____

L

—lake's
—language
—lateness
—law
—leader
—least
—let's
—letting
—level
—libraries
—lie
—life
—little
—lives

—located
—lunches

_____
_____
_____
_____

M

—machine
—mark
—married
—matter
—maybe
—measure
—meet
—memories
—million
—minute
—misbehaved
—misheard
—misplaced
—Miss
—misspelled

—misunderstanding
—mixed
—modern
—moment
—morning
—mountain
—mouthful
—Mr.
—Mrs.
—Ms.

_____
_____
_____
_____
_____
_____
_____
_____

N

—nation's
—nations'
—nature
—neighbor

Dictionary and Personal Word List

__neither

__never

__noise

__nonfiction

__nonhuman

__nonreturnable

__notice

_____

_____

_____

_____

_____

_____

O

__ocean

__of course

__off

__office

__open

__order

__ourselves

_____

_____

_____

P

__parents

__party

__period

__person

__physical

__picture

__plain

__plastic

__police

__pond

__population

__potatoes

__power

__precooked

__pregame

__preseason

__president

__priced

__probably

__problem

__produce

__program

__prove

__provided

__public

__purpose

_____

_____

_____

_____

_____

_____

_____

Q

__question

__quieter

__quitting

_____

_____

R

__reason

__receive

__recharge

__recycle

__remembered

— replaceable
— replied
— restudy
— result
— return
— room
— round

_____
_____
_____
_____
_____

S

— saved
— science
— scrubbed
— second
— secret
— section
— separate
— serious
— serve
— setting
— several

— sheep
— shook
— shore
— shoulder
— shown
— shy
— side
— single
— size
— skills
— skipped
— slightly
— smiling
— soil
— solve
— space
— special
— spend
— splitting
— spoke
— sprayed
— spread
— start
— stones'
— stories

— streets'
— strike
— student
— sudden
— sugar
— summer
— supplies
— surface

_____
_____
_____
_____
_____
_____
_____
_____
_____
_____
_____
_____
_____

Dictionary and Personal Word List

Name: _____

T

___ table
___ tasteless
___ taught
___ teacher
___ teeth
___ television
___ temperature
___ terrible
___ those
___ though
___ thoughtful
___ thousand
___ threw
___ through
___ tiniest
___ today's
___ together
___ tonight
___ tool
___ total
___ touch
___ tracks
___ traded
___ traffic

___ travel
___ tree's
___ trees'
___ tube
___ type

_____
_____
_____
_____
_____
_____
_____
_____
_____

U

___ understood
___ unforgettable
___ unimportant
___ uninteresting
___ unless
___ unnumbered
___ until
___ unusual

___ upon
___ used to

_____
_____
_____
_____

V

___ valley
___ vegetables
___ view
___ village

_____
_____

W

___ wanted
___ washable
___ wasting
___ waving
___ weigh
___ weight
___ were
___ what
___ whenever

Name:

___ where

___ whether

___ wife

___ window

___ wireless

___ wives

___ women's

___ won

___ wonder

___ won't

___ wool

___ worry

___ written

___ wrote

X, Y, Z

___ year's

___ yellow

___ young

Spelling References

Single-syllable Doubling Generalization

IF the base word has

- one syllable,
- one vowel,
- and one consonant after the vowel

AND the suffix begins with a vowel,

THEN double the last consonant.

Examples

stop + ing = stopping   sun + y = sunny

big + est = biggest   hid + en = hidden

Drop e Generalization

IF the base word ends with consonant-**e**

AND the suffix begins with a vowel,

THEN drop **e**.

Examples

ride + ing = riding   brave + est = bravest

write + er = writer   shine + y = shiny

Change y to i Generalization

IF the base word ends with consonant-**y**
AND the suffix begins with any letter except **i**,
THEN change **y** to **i**.

Examples

puppy + es = puppies   happy + ness = happiness

carry + ed = carried   beauty + ful = beautiful

Polysyllabic Doubling Generalization

IF the base word is polysyllabic
   – and ends with one vowel and one consonant
   – and has the accent on the last syllable
AND the suffix begins with a vowel,
THEN double the last consonant.

Examples

begin + ing = beginning   begin + er = beginner

admit + ed = admitted   forgot + en = forgotten

Frequently Misspelled Words

Name:

The phrases in parentheses will help you choose the correct word. Contractions and compound word families are shown on page 187.

A
all ready (*They are all ready.*)
all right
a lot

B
because
before
believe
buy (*She will buy a pen.*)

C
cannot
classroom
clothes

D, E, F
Dr.
eighteen
eighty
field
first
forty
fourth (*third and fourth*)
friend

G, H, I
guess
hear (*I can hear you.*)
heard

J, K, L
loose (*The knot came loose.*)
lose (*Don't lose your pen.*)

M, N, O
men's
Miss
Mr.
Mrs.
Ms.
off
one (*There's one page left.*)

P, Q, R
people
quite

S
school
sense
St. (*Main St.; St. Louis*)

T, U, V
their (*Join their group.*)
there (*There it is.*)
thirty
thought
through (*Wind blew through the window.*)
too (*I ran too fast. I like that book, too.*)

touch
truth
two (*We ate two oranges.*)
used to

W, X, Y, Z
wanted
weather (*sunny weather*)
were
what
where
whether (*He asked whether he could go.*)
while
whole (*the whole book*)
wind (*The wind blew. Wind up the string.*)
women
would (*Yes, I would.*)

Name: _____

CONTRACTIONS

n't (not)	's (is, has)	'll (will, shall)	'd (would, had)	've (have)	're (are)	'm (am) 's (us)
aren't	here's	he'll	he'd	I've	they're	I'm
can't	he's	I'll	I'd	you've	we're	let's
couldn't	how's	it'll	she'd	we've	you're	
didn't	it's	she'll	they'd	they've		
doesn't	she's	that'll	we'd			
don't	that's	they'll	who'd			
hadn't	there's	we'll	you'd			
hasn't	what's	you'll				
haven't	where's					
isn't	who's					
mustn't						
shouldn't						
wasn't						
weren't						
won't						
wouldn't						

COMPOUND WORD FAMILIES

no-	any-	some-	every-	-ever
nobody	anybody	somebody	everybody	forever
nowhere	anyone	somehow	everyone	however
	anything	someone	everything	whatever
	anyway	something	everywhere	whenever
	anywhere	sometime		
		sometimes		
		somewhat		
		somewhere		